POSTCARD HISTORY SERIES

Resorts of Riverside County

WOMAN AT BEAUTY SPRING, MURRIETA HOT SPRINGS, *C.* 1910. What better way to advertise "Beauty Spring" than with a beautiful girl about to partake of the liquid offerings at Guenther's Murrieta Hot Springs resort. Many of Riverside County's resorts catered to those hoping to revive themselves or cure an ailment by the use of mineral waters from many different springs.

POSTCARD HISTORY SERIES

Resorts of Riverside County

Steve Lech

ARCADIA

ISBN 0-7385-3078-6

Published by Arcadia Publishing
Charleston SC, Chicago IL, Portsmouth NH, San Francisco CA

Printed in Great Britain

Library of Congress Catalog Card Number: 2005931514

For all general information contact Arcadia Publishing at:
Telephone 843-853-2070
Fax 843-853-0044
E-mail sales@arcadiapublishing.com
For customer service and orders:
Toll-Free 1-888-313-2665

Visit us on the internet at http://www.arcadiapublishing.com

Contents

ACKNOWLEDGMENTS

As popular as the resorts of Riverside County were, information about them is woefully inadequate—few people thought to preserve much information about what is shown in this book. Therefore, I am especially indebted to the following people for providing me with both research material and insight into some of the places outlined in this work. I'd like to thank Ruth Atkins for finding information relative to Elsinore and some of its resorts; Beti An Hynes for tracking down information in Perris and for putting me in touch with Norman Hughes, to whom I'm greatly indebted for his knowledge of early Perris; Phil Brigandi for once again opening his extensive files, this time regarding the resorts in the San Jacinto area; and finally Elizabeth and Kitty Kieley for sitting down with me and setting me straight on the intricacies of the old Desert Inn and Palm Springs in general. Without the generous assistance of all of the people mentioned here, this book would not be what it is.

INTRODUCTION

Riverside County is a vast area of more than 7,200 square miles, stretching from the Santa Ana Mountains on the west to the Colorado River on the east. Throughout most of its history, Riverside County generally has been known as an agricultural wonderland, producing everything from navel oranges to apricots, wine grapes, cherries, and the exotic date. However, few people living today realize that there was another facet to Riverside County's popularity from about the 1880s to the 1960s. During that time, numerous resorts dotted the landscape, offering rest, relaxation, activities, and even recuperation to thousands of people both local and far away.

The resorts of Riverside County came in many varieties. The ones best remembered today are the many hot springs resorts. These resorts, located along the myriad of faults that traverse the county, offered hot and cold mineral waters to their guests, most of whom were helped, or at least thought they were helped, by soaking in and drinking these natural waters. Resorts such as Glen Ivy, Murrieta, Eden, Gilman, Soboba, and Desert Hot Springs offered a way for people to "take the waters" while basking in the climate of Southern California.

Another form of resort was the medical resort, or sanitarium. These places generally catered to people coming from the east with lung problems. In the days before the widespread use of antibiotics, people with asthma, bronchitis, or the dreaded tuberculosis were often told to seek a warmer and dryer climate to find a cure. Places such as the Idyllwild Sanitarium, Glen Ivy Hot Springs, the Indio depot/hotel, and the Desert Inn in Palm Springs opened to help these people but soon found more lucrative business in catering to a general population instead of the "one-lungers," as they were known.

Finally, there were many resort and/or different sized hotels that offered relaxation to visitors who simply wanted a vacation in the Southern California climate. It may seem odd to people today, but simply going to a nice hotel where one could relax, enjoy the climate, and get away from home was a perfectly enjoyable vacation to many people at the time. This is why places like the Mission Inn in Riverside, the Robertine in Perris, the San Gorgonio Inn in Banning, and the Vosburg Hotel in San Jacinto are included in this book.

All of the postcard views shown in this book come from my personal collection of some 2,500 views of Riverside County and date to a time when most correspondence was done not by phone or e-mail, but by letter or picture postcard. These postcards offered an inexpensive way for people to show where they had been and to tell their friends and loved ones about the places they'd visited. Because it was a truly special occasion to visit many of the places shown here, a significant number of the postcards were kept by people and remain a fairly easy way to enjoy history today. Luckily for us, many of these cards were saved in collections.

It is my hope that this book will give some idea that Riverside County was truly a place that many people enjoyed visiting. These resorts were often visited for several days, weeks, or even months at a time, and oftentimes the senders of these postcards commented on how beautiful the area was. When you look at these views, note the fact that many of them were surrounded by vast open areas, which helped to give a sense that the visitor was "getting away from it all."

Unfortunately, most of the views shown in this book can no longer be recreated. Differences in how people vacation, the drying up of many of the hot springs, and rampant, unchecked, and visually offensive development that has destroyed many of our vistas have all contributed to the decline of most of the places and views shown here. Still, though, some do exist and can be enjoyed.

Please keep in mind that due to space requirements, I have de-emphasized the Mission Inn in Riverside and Palm Springs in general. It's not meant as a slight, but I showed several Mission Inn postcard views in my *Riverside in Vintage Postcards* book, and a separate book has been published by Arcadia on *Palm Springs in Vintage Postcards*. With this in mind, I hope you find this excursion into an aspect of Riverside County's past as fascinating as I have.

One

NORTHWEST
RIVERSIDE, NORCO, TEMESCAL, AND PERRIS

OVERALL VIEW OF THE MISSION INN, C. 1912. The Mission Inn is the best-known resort hotel in Riverside County. The Mission Inn was opened by Frank Miller in 1903 and continued to be a driving force in Riverside's development for 50 years. The quote from David Starr Jordan says it all—Frank Miller's hotel was one that "a Californian can recognize as his own."

MISSION INN COURTYARD, CAMPANILE, AND PERGOLA, *C.* 1905. Many postcards showed various scenes of the Mission Inn courtyard. This view shows the pergola (vine-covered structure on the right), constructed as a shaded walkway around the courtyard. Also visible is the Campanile, or Mission-style bell tower that heralded guests to the main entrance of the hotel. On the left is the old Miller family home, known as the "Old Adobe."

CARMEL TOWER DRAWING, 1911. This view is of the Cloister Wing at Sixth and Orange Streets and shows the second wing to be added to the hotel. The quote indicates that the buttresses fronting Orange Street were patterned after the San Gabriel Mission and that the Carmel Tower was inspired by the Carmel Mission Chapel. Some of the earliest references call this portion a monastery, as shown here.

SPANISH ART GALLERY, MID-1920S. This is the Spanish Art Gallery, the largest room in the Spanish wing. In 1914, Frank Miller added this third wing to the hotel after having visited Spain and becoming enamored with Spanish art and architecture. The Spanish Art Gallery displayed Miller's ever-growing collection of artwork from abroad. One very recognizable artifact appears in the center of this shot—the William Keith painting entitled *California Alps* that hangs near the front desk today.

THE MISSION INN ROTUNDA, 1932. The Rotunda, located at the corner of Sixth and Main Streets, was completed in 1931 by G. Stanley Wilson and was the last portion of the hotel to be built. Designed to be the commercial portion of the hotel, this structure housed several professional offices and was decorated with emblems of many countries. Its tall, winding staircase has been used for many wedding pictures and movies.

ANCHORAGE PARK INN AND GROUNDS, *C.* 1915–1920. This small private resort was developed around the home of Riverside pioneer Ebenezer Brown. Brown and Dr. James Greves had been the first of John North's contingency to view the land that would become Riverside. Once Riverside was established, Brown filed for approximately 100 acres of land about a half mile northeast of Riverside (about where the I-215/60 interchange is today) and here built his home, which he called "the Anchorage." Soon afterward, he established an orange grove and nursery and expanded the home into a small hotel. He landscaped the grounds, which included the Riverside Upper Canal, used as a centerpiece of the grounds. In 1890, it was said that 30 people could be accommodated. By the 1930s, the hotel had closed.

LAKE NORCONIAN CLUB (SOUTHERN VIEW), *c.* 1930. The establishment of the Lake Norconian Club happened quite by accident. In early 1925, Rex B. Clark of the North Corona Land Company (hence Norco) had a crew drilling irrigation wells. One of the crews struck a hot sulphur spring, and Clark immediately decided to build a world-class hotel and resort around it. Clark hired architect Dwight Gibbs to design the hotel, which was built starting in 1927. On February 2, 1929, the Lake Norconian Club opened with an all-day affair, including lunch, sporting events, an extravagant dinner, and a night of dancing. At the time, it was heralded as one of Southern California's best pleasure resorts.

LAKE NORCONIAN CLUB (NORTHERN VIEW), ***C.*** **1930.** Costing nearly $4 million to construct, the Lake Norconian Club was a marvel of Mediterranean architecture. The main building housed 120 guest rooms along with the lobby, parlors, and lounging, dining, and ballrooms. Hot sulphur water from the nearby springs was piped into special bathing rooms and a large swimming plunge. In addition to the inside amenities, the grounds boasted of terraced gardens, an 18-hole golf course, and several miles of hiking/riding trails.

LAKE NORCONIAN, CASINO/BOATHOUSE, AND HOTEL, c. 1930. This view shows all of the portions of the club, the Lake Norconian in the foreground, the combination casino and boathouse along the lakeside, and the main hotel building in the background.

LAKE NORCONIAN CLUB AS NAVAL HOSPITAL, c. 1942. Unfortunately for Rex Clark, the Great Depression hit just months after the opening of his Lake Norconian Club. Throughout the 1930s, the club never truly became profitable. Late in 1941, at the onset of World War II, the navy bought the resort from Clark and converted it into a hospital, as shown here.

GLEN IVY HOT SPRINGS ENTRANCE, MID-1920S. The benefits of the naturally occurring mineral hot springs located in the Temescal Canyon have been known for hundreds, if not thousands, of years. Although commercial use of the hot springs began by September 1860, when it was known as Temescal Hot Springs, it was not until 1890 when then-owners Mr. and Mrs. W. G. Steers named it Glen Ivy. The year 1913 saw ownership of the springs transfer to Frank and Mabel Johnson, who soon developed it into the resort shown above and in many of the following views. After 25 years of running the resort successfully, they sold the property to Danish hotelman Axel Springborg, who continued the tradition for nearly 30 years more. Extensive advertising by both the Johnsons and Springborg, combined with unmatched hospitality, made Glen Ivy Hot Springs one of Riverside County's premier resorts.

MAIN DRIVE, GLEN IVY HOT SPRINGS, MID-1920S. A palm-tree lined drive was an exotic element to people living in the Midwest or on the East Coast, and this view shows the one at Glen Ivy full of mature palm trees. Undoubtedly this gave the receiver a sense of the tropical warmth that awaited him in Southern California.

VIEW OF GLEN IVY FROM DRIVE, 1920S. This is the view that would have greeted guests to Glen Ivy as they arrived in the 1920s.

THE TAVERN, GLEN IVY HOT SPRINGS, MID-1930S. The Tavern was the reception and hotel building for the resort. This card was sent to a couple who had just visited. It states that "we were happy to welcome you to Glen Ivy—we trust your stay was thoroughly enjoyed and we hope to welcome you often.—The Springborgs."

ANOTHER VIEW OF THE TAVERN, GLEN IVY HOT SPRINGS, 1920S. This view greeted guests upon arrival. The Tavern was constructed around and included portions of the adobe hotel that dated to 1876. Along with many other buildings, the Tavern was completed in the summer of 1923 by Frank Johnson.

Relaxing at Glen Ivy Hot Springs, 1920s. One of the main themes of Glen Ivy, and the myriad other resorts throughout Southern California, was relaxation. Here we see a guest relaxing on the porch of the Tavern overlooking the grounds of Glen Ivy.

View from Main Building, Glen Ivy Hot Springs, 1920s. Even man's best friend could find relaxation at Glen Ivy. Many postcards showed garden areas and other "tropical views" to entice Easterners west for a visit.

AMERICAN INDIAN FIREPLACE, GLEN IVY TAVERN, MID-1920S. This imposing fireplace was constructed using some of the many American Indian artifacts found on the Glen Ivy site. This would have been a unique and interesting feature to many visitors in the early years.

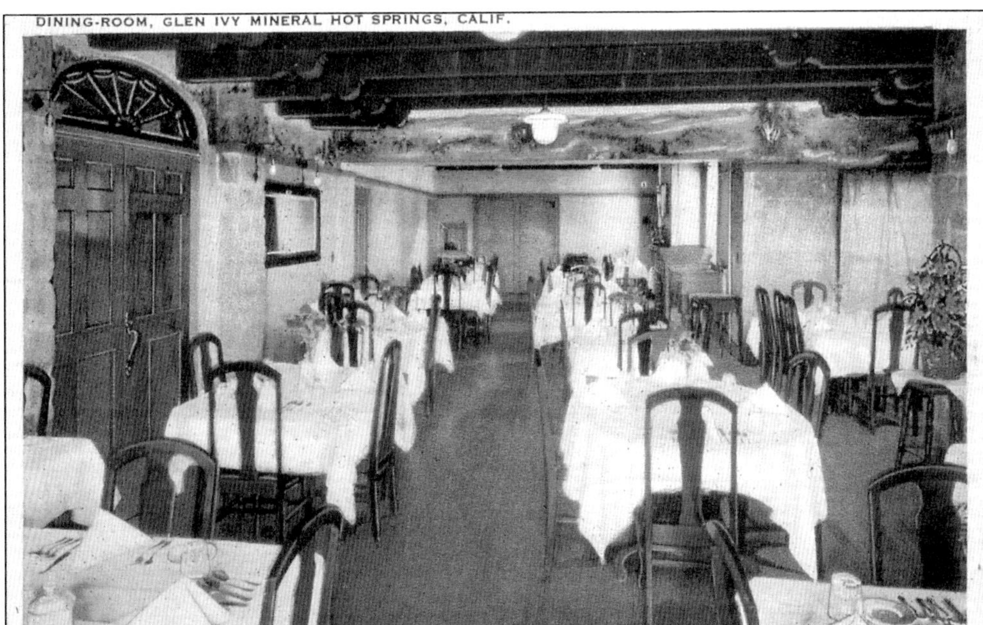

DINING ROOM, GLEN IVY HOT SPRINGS, LATE 1920S. Since the object of a resort was to have people spend several days or weeks at a time, dining facilities were important and were featured on postcards to show others what awaited them. The room pictured above was located in the Tavern.

BATHHOUSE, GLEN IVY HOT SPRINGS, 1920S. This building, erected by Frank Johnson late in 1927, contained "Roman tubs and rooms of imported tile. Steam and electric baths, Sun Baths, Massage and Hydro-Therapy in all its forms. Mineral Baths together with the massage treatment are recognized as a successful treatment for rheumatism, neuritis, and other nervous disorders."

WARM SULPHUR PLUNGE, GLEN IVY HOT SPRINGS, MID-1920S. This building was part of the 1923 upgrade of the resort and enclosed what had been a swimming hole for many decades. By the mid-1920s, this building was termed "a sanitary warm Sulphur water swimming plunge amidst beautiful surroundings." This tile building measured 85 feet by 35 feet.

SWIMMING POOL, GLEN IVY HOT SPRINGS, *c.* 1940. In the late 1930s, yet another attraction was added to Glen Ivy—the swimming pool. By this time, swimming pools were becoming a "must have" for resorts and hotels, and despite the fact that there were many places in which to get wet, Glen Ivy added its pool.

THE SPRING HOUSE, GLEN IVY HOT SPRINGS, 1920S. The Spring House was one of many little nooks where one could enjoy some quiet time in the outdoors. What better place to read a book or write a postcard back home while gazing out among the "tropical" scenery?

TWO VIEWS OF COTTAGES, GLEN IVY HOT SPRINGS, 1920S. These two views show some of the cottages available for rent. People who wanted more privacy could stay in an individual cottage instead of the hotel. One guest remarked, "If you want to take a little trip, do come to this delightful spot—it is a fascinating place for rest. I am feeling so much better."

COLDWATER CANYON, GLEN IVY HOT SPRINGS, EARLY 1920S. Part of the allure of visiting a place such as Glen Ivy was the opportunity to "get back to nature." One visitor described the surrounding area thusly: "Cold Water Canyon, a Sylvan retreat, cool and fragrant, tempts and beckons to the traveler. Live oaks, sycamores, and cottonwoods dot the countryside, while along the mountain slopes a few pines march bravely skyward."

LIVE OAKS, GLEN IVY HOT SPRINGS, EARLY 1920S. Walkways like this offered a perfect place to rest, relax, or recuperate, although Glen Ivy specifically forbid people with infectious diseases. This type of postcard sought to show would-be visitors the scenery that awaited them at the resort.

Hotel Robertine, Perris, c. 1908. The Hotel Robertine was a small cottage-type hotel located at the southwest corner of Fifth and C Streets in Perris. The building on the right was the dining room, the one on the left, the sleeping quarters. Owned at times by Miss V. A. Lawrence and Mrs. Katherine O'Grady, the Hotel Robertine was a franchise operation, not unlike the famed Harvey Houses of the time. Henry Harford, later a Perris realtor and landowner for whom Harford Springs is named, arrived at the Robertine from the East with little chance of recuperating from lung problems. His month-long stay at the Robertine convinced him to move to Perris, where he spent the rest of his life.

El Perrisito Resort, Perris, Late 1920s. The El Perrisito Resort was located in the foothills just west of downtown Perris, overlooking the Perris Valley. El Perrisito was advertised as "the desert resort located nearest Los Angeles. . . Radio active water—swimming in 60 foot tile plunge, tennis—horseback riding and hiking over miles of private bridle paths and trails through thousand acres of desert estates, in high and dry desert air, 1500 feet in altitude, invigorating climate. A 'never-to-be-forgotten' panorama of awe-inspiring views." By the mid-1930s, the resort had folded, and the building housed the Palomar Boys School.

Two

SOUTHWEST
ELSINORE AND MURRIETA

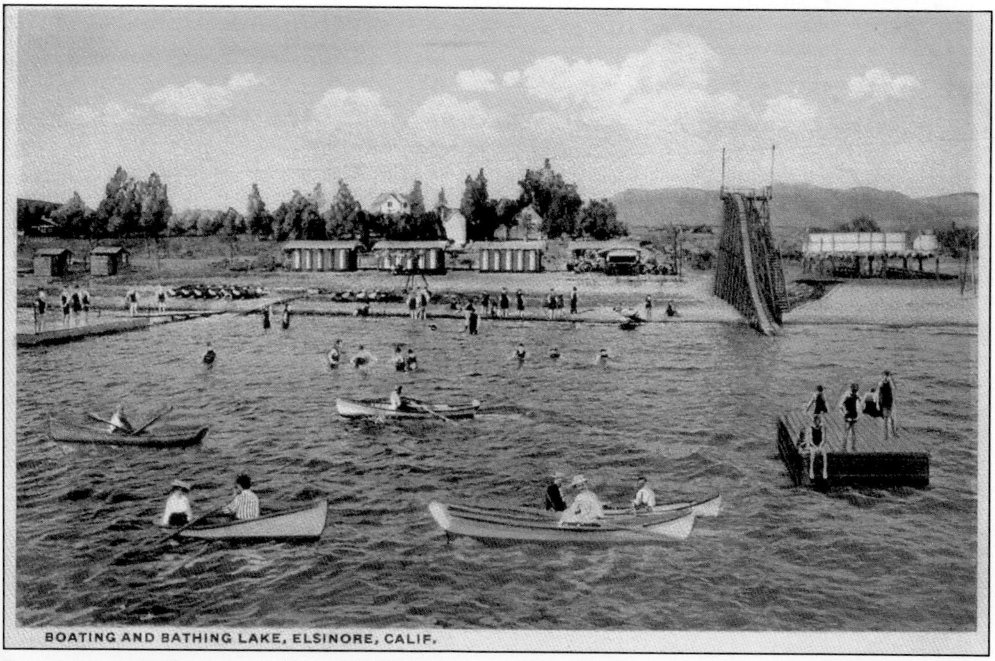

BOATING AND BATHING, LAKE ELSINORE, *C.* 1915. Elsinore has been a popular resort town since its inception in the early 1880s. Known for recreation on and around the lake, plus the many hot springs hotels and resorts contained within the city, Elsinore remained popular for years. Here visitors enjoy boat rides near the bathing facilities.

LAKE VIEW INN, ELSINORE, 1920S. This building opened early in 1895 under the direction of Dr. H. C. Royer and C. S. Traphagan and replaced the Lake Dale Hotel, constructed in 1886, that had burned. It sat on a knoll at the corner of Spring and Limited Streets and commanded a wide view of Lake Elsinore and the surrounding valley. It catered to many of the sportsmen who visited Elsinore.

CRESCENT BATHHOUSE (ELSINORE HOT SPRINGS), 1908. This Elsinore landmark, located at the corner of Spring and Graham Streets, was built in 1887 as a bathhouse for the original hot springs. Frank Ferris designed the unique building that was used as the main bathhouse for the Lake Dale (later Lake View) Hotel. Note the railroad tracks in the foreground—Elsinore's railroad station was just behind the photographer.

Bathing at Elsinore Hot Springs, c. 1910. This is one of the many bathing facilities that were available in the Crescent Bathhouse. "The hot mineral water is unsurpassed for the cure of disease . . . the large bathing establishment is said by all who have seen it to be the finest to be found in the State. . . Invalids often regain their health here after having tried various other places, which should encourage those who have stubborn maladies and are seeking help," indicated one advertisement from 1895.

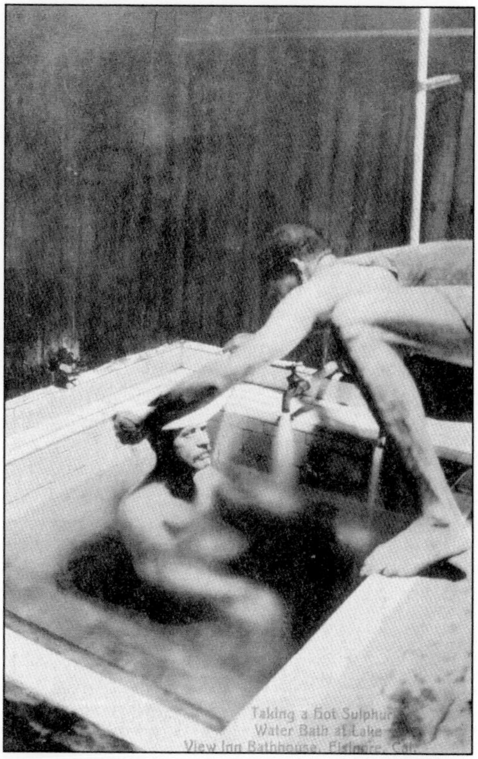

Clevelin Country Club, Lake Elsinore, c. 1930. The Clevelin Country Club, also known as the Lake Elsinore Country Club, was a popular beachfront resort that opened in 1928. It was a Clevelin Realty Company development and boasted of a ballroom, apartments, dining room, bar, sleeping rooms, and banquet/meeting rooms.

CLEVELIN COUNTRY CLUB AND PIER, *c.* 1930. One of the drawing cards to the Clevelin Country Club was its pier, which extended into the lake. Constructed in 1926, it was improved by the addition of a second story, as shown here in 1927. This addition was necessary due to the abundant rains that had flooded the lake, making the lower pier unusable.

ALOHA PIER, LAKE ELSINORE, LATE 1920S. The Aloha Pier was constructed adjacent to the one of the Clevelin group but was better known in the early days. It was from the Aloha Pier that many boat races began. The group shown above, though, is obviously out for a party on the lake.

ALOHA PIER, LATE 1920S. This view is from the dance floor of the Aloha Pier, where dances were held generally during the summer. Note the boathouse to the right and some of the better homes above the lake. The Aloha and Clevelin Piers added to the resort experience at Elsinore and helped in the many real estate ventures.

BUNDY HOTEL AND HOT SPRINGS, ELSINORE, *c.* 1908. In 1886, the Bundy family built this facility along Spring Street between Sumner and West Heald Streets. By the time of this photograph, several other buildings, including cottages and bathhouses, had been constructed. By 1904, the Bundys had left, selling the facility to Mr. and Mrs. O. W. Amsbury, who kept the old hotel name for several years.

NEW AMSBURY HOTEL AND BATHHOUSE, ELSINORE, *c.* 1920. In 1919, the Amsbury family expanded their operation by building a new, hollow-tile facility directly across Spring Street from the old hotel. It was said that the hollow tiles "do much to assure a pleasant temperature the year around." One guest summed up her stay, "I am here for a week of lazy rest and am enjoying it immensely!"

CRESWELL HOT MINERAL BATHS, ELSINORE, MID-1920S. The spring that was tapped for this facility was originally called the "Dutchman's Well" and was said to be flowing before the settlement of Elsinore. After a succession of owners, a Captain Cresswell bought it and is said to have built the building shown above, probably in the mid-1910s. The Creswell Bathhouse was one of many such facilities in Elsinore, where, according to one article, "the curative water, coming up hot from the earth, is piped to the bath and treatment rooms, where skilled attendants care for the hundreds of annual patients."

Panoramic View, Guenther's Murrieta Hot Springs, c. 1906. Murrieta Hot Springs has been a popular place for relaxation and healing for thousands of years. Known as Cherukanukna Hakiwuna by the Luiseno Indians, the springs were first advertised to settlers in the 1870s. Beginning then, a series of owners ran various camp-style resorts at the springs. By the turn of the century, though, more cattle were using the waters than people, since the owners of the

property were interested mainly in ranching and not developing the springs. That changed in 1902 when German-born immigrant Fritz Guenther purchased the springs and began to develop what would become one of Riverside County's better-known resorts. The view pictured above shows the springs after many of Guenther's improvements had unfolded.

GROUP AT THE "FOUNTAIN OF YOUTH" SPRING, MURRIETA HOT SPRINGS, *C.* 1909. The Fountain of Youth Spring, or simply the Big Spring or Siloam, was the largest of the springs at Murrieta Hot Springs. This fed water to several areas of the resort. The waters were said to heal many ailments, although sometimes they didn't always agree with the person. "This is a nice morning. I can't say that I feel better yet but feel much worse altho I haven't any doubt that I will be cured. The fact that I feel worse is only a sign that it is working on me," wrote one person from the resort in September 1910.

SPRING WATER RESERVOIR, MURRIETA HOT SPRINGS, EARLY 1920S. Showing the main reservoir, this view is directly opposite the one on the previous page. Used for water storage, the pool was also a picturesque photograph location, enticing visitors who may have otherwise thought of Southern California as a vast desert.

SHADE PAVILION, MURRIETA HOT SPRINGS, *C.* 1910. This view looks toward the spring water reservoir shown in the previous two views. The reservoir is visible to the right of center. Also visible here are some of the cabins and the mud bathhouse. "I am feeling better now. Mamma went home today but I will stay 10 days longer," wrote one guest.

Group Assembled at Spring Water Reservoir, Murrieta Hot Springs, c. 1909. Note how the group pictured here is framed by tule and palm fronds. This was considered very tropical, especially to Easterners who had never seen such foliage. Also note that each of the members of the group has a drinking ladle and is ready to "taste the waters."

Original Bathhouses, Murrieta Hot Springs, c. 1905. These buildings served for many years as bathhouses where guests could come to bathe in the waters. Typically each room was small enough for one person and had a small deep-set tile tub with stairs that led down into the waters. The bathhouses were strictly divided by gender.

MUD BATHHOUSE, MURRIETA HOT SPRINGS, *C.* 1904. This new mud bathhouse, completed in 1903, was one of the first improvements made by Fritz Guenther once he assumed ownership of the resort in 1902. The building was designed to accommodate several people wanting to soak in the mineral-rich mud.

MUD BATHHOUSES, MURRIETA HOT SPRINGS, *C.* 1910. After just a few years, additions were made to the original mud bathhouse, and others were added to accommodate the ever-growing number of guests coming to the resort.

MAIN GUEST BUILDINGS, MURRIETA HOT SPRINGS, *C.* 1905. The two buildings shown here include the main office and dining hall (right) and the original Monterey Hotel in the background, which date to 1903 and 1904 respectively. Although the springs had been known for centuries, it was Fritz Guenther who developed Murrieta Hot Springs into a true resort. He was very familiar with the hot springs resorts he had seen in Europe and patterned his new resort after many of them. The accommodations seen above would have been considered first rate in the early 1900s, and this recognition helped to propel Murrieta Hot Springs into becoming one of the foremost hot springs resorts in California, if not the western United States.

"A FEW OF OUR GUESTS," MURRIETA HOT SPRINGS, *C.* 1909. The guests are seated and standing in front of the main office building, which also housed the dining room. Going to a resort such as Murrieta Hot Springs was truly a special occasion for many of the visitors, and it was quite customary to have a photograph taken somewhere on the grounds.

DINING HALL, MURRIETA HOT SPRINGS, *C.* 1905. The dining hall served as both dining area and assembly area for awhile. Guests of the resort ate all of their meals here, and there was a staff of professional cooks and others to wait on them. Note the pipes that are supplying gas to the gas-light fixtures.

TYPICAL TENT CABIN, MURRIETA HOT SPRINGS, c. 1906. In an era when people often slept outside for their health, open-style tent cabins such as the one shown above were quite popular at resorts like Murrieta Hot Springs. These tent cabins, which rented for $10 per week, dated to the previous owners, and Guenther soon replaced many of them with hard-sided cabins.

ROW OF CAMPING COTTAGES, MURRIETA HOT SPRINGS, c. 1906. Cottages, such as those shown above, housed the majority of guests at the resort in the early days. Although cramped by today's standards, these cabins were a "home away from home" to people who came out hoping to spend a week or two relaxing and partaking of the curative waters offered by the springs.

COTTAGE ROW, MURRIETA HOT SPRINGS, *C.* 1904. Cottage row was a very early improvement at the resort. Finished in 1903, Cottage Row represented a step up from the tent camping seen previously. The units were larger, and they were solid, unlike the canvas-sided tents. These typically rented for about $12 per week.

COTTAGE ROW AND PALM LANE, MURRIETA HOT SPRINGS, *C.* 1909. This view shows a different angle of Cottage Row, ending at the mud bathhouses in the center of the picture. The palm trees were indicative of the "tropical" experience to be had at the resort. Cottage Row was in existence for almost 60 years when it was torn down in the early 1960s to make way for more improvements.

CALIFORNIA HOTEL, MURRIETA HOT SPRINGS, *c.* 1912. The almost instant popularity of Guenther's Murrieta Hot Springs prompted many improvements in the early years. One of these was the new, larger California Hotel, which was completed in 1908. This facility increased the resort's capacity greatly and catered to a more sophisticated crowd not content to be housed in a canvas or wood cottage during their stay.

DAIRY STOCK, MURRIETA HOT SPRINGS, *c.* 1912. The Guenthers had a herd of pure-bred Holstein cows that lived on-site. Most meals in the dining hall were accompanied by pitchers of fresh whole milk and buttermilk from this herd.

GARAGE, MURRIETA HOT SPRINGS, *C.* 1912. A truly novel pastime during the early 20th century was an automobile trip. Fritz Guenther accommodated his guests by providing automobiles for that purpose. The truck in the middle of the picture was used to shuttle guests to and from the Murrieta train station and Guenther's resort. It was simply a truck to which seats were added for guests.

BIG SPRINGS PAVILION, MURRIETA HOT SPRINGS, *C.* 1933. In 1932, the former Big Springs reservoir was bricked over and made into the shaded pavilion pictured here. Note the well-like structure in the middle. It was open to the springs so guests could come by and dip their dipper into it and drink the mineral-laden waters. "Had a fine time yesterday. Taking baths, drinking sulphur water, out hunting."

NEW BUILDINGS AND AREA LANDMARKS, MURRIETA HOT SPRINGS, LATE 1920S. The larger views in these two postcards show the new bathhouse (above) completed in 1928 and the hotel annex (below) completed in March 1926. Both of these buildings were concrete and designed in a Spanish style of architecture. The other scenes show area landmarks that could be visited while at the resort, such as Lake Elsinore, the original Temecula ranch (Wolf store), and the Wolf monument.

TYPICAL GUEST ROOM, MURRIETA HOT SPRINGS, LATE 1920S. This modern, well-appointed room was typical of what would greet the prospective guest as he or she arrived in the new hotel annex. Fairly small by today's standards, this was considered quite comfortable at the time, especially given the fact that most of the guests' time was spent either in the baths, lounging by the pool, or engaging in any of the other activities available to them.

LOBBY OF THE HOTEL ANNEX, MURRIETA HOT SPRINGS, LATE 1920S. As this view shows, Murrieta Hot Springs had "come of age" by the late 1920s with the addition of the new hotel annex. This portion of the resort was well equipped to handle more discriminating customers like the sender of this card, who wrote to her friend in Winslow, Arizona, to let her know that she was recovering at Murrieta Hot Springs from a bout of laryngitis.

TENNIS COURTS AND POPULAR SPORTS, MURRIETA HOT SPRINGS. Because of the Guenther's desire to make Murrieta Hot Springs a health-oriented resort, sports and other physical activities were included almost from the beginning. Hiking, tennis, riding, and, of course, swimming, were some of the many activities for guests. In the above view, three people pose in front of the tennis courts *c.* 1930. In the below postcard, many of the activities available to guests are shown, *c.* 1945.

DANCE HALL AND ORCHESTRA, MURRIETA HOT SPRINGS, MID-1920S. Dances were a popular form of entertainment for resort visitors, and Murrieta Hot Springs was no exception. This view shows the Memorial Auditorium (dedicated to the memory of Fritz Guenther) decorated for such an occasion, along with the resort's staff band.

AMUSEMENT AUDITORIUM, MURRIETA HOT SPRINGS, *C.* 1930. The amusement auditorium was a small area set aside for quiet games, conversation, relaxation, or getting a drink, as shown by the barstools in the lower left. This area provided less rigorous activities for guests to while away the hours.

GROUP AT PAINTED ROCK, MURRIETA HOT SPRINGS, C. 1904. Painted Rock was a series of American Indian petroglyphs painted and inscribed onto the rocks near the resort. A short hike from the main facility would bring the visitor to Painted Rock, which was a favorite outing site among guests. These excursionists are sunning themselves among the petroglyphs, which are visible especially in the lower left of the picture.

FORTY NINER ROOM, MURRIETA HOT SPRINGS, C. 1965. This bar and lounge began as the Frontier Bar in 1933 after the repeal of prohibition. The simple bar and lounge was a staple among resorts, hotels, and clubhouses beginning in the 1930s, and Murrieta Hot Springs was no different. In the 1950s, the Frontier Bar was renamed the Forty Niner Room and was located in the main auditorium.

Three

San Gorgonio Pass
Banning and Beaumont

Highland Home, c. 1910. In 1884, a group of investors purchased the ranch of Pioneer Pass resident Dr. Isaac Smith, who had lived there since 1853. Here they built the three-story structure shown above and opened it as the Highland Home, a resort in the foothills above Beaumont. The writer of this card assured her friend in Covina, "There are so many places of interest to see . . . this place certainly has a great future."

MAIN BUILDING, HIGHLAND SPRINGS RESORT, 1930S–1940S. In August 1927, brothers Fred and William Hirsch purchased the Highland Home. Over the next several years, they modernized the resort, added to it, and constructed the main building, seen in these two views. The one above dates to the early 1930s, and shows the Federal-style building that became the centerpiece of the resort. The below view dates to the mid-1940s and shows additions.

COTTAGES, HIGHLAND SPRINGS RESORT, 1930S. Many resorts of this time housed guests in individual cottages, and the Highland Springs Resort was no exception. Because people tended to stay for a week or longer, having just a room was not as desirable.

COTTAGES, HIGHLAND SPRINGS RESORT, 1930S. This is a view of different cottages, more in keeping with the Federal-style main building. It was the desire of the resort operators to have their facility feel just like home.

HIGHLAND SPRINGS RESORT GROUNDS, EARLY 1930S. This view shows some of the nearly 500 acres eventually encompassed by Highland Springs. The swimming pool is to the left of center, and on the far right are a series of picnic tables. Views such as this one were important for showing the amenities offered by the resort to prospective guests.

HIGHLAND SPRINGS MINERAL BATHS, LATE 1930S. Despite its name, the Highland Springs Resort was more of a dude ranch and relaxation resort than a hot springs. This card, however, showed the prospective guest the mineral baths that awaited should he or she care to partake. The writer of this card told his friend in Los Angeles that "this place is a regular spa—Nauheim baths and everything, plus beautiful surroundings and a bracing climate. Good food too!"

SWIMMING POOL, HIGHLAND SPRINGS RESORT. Compared to today, swimming pools were a relative rarity in the 1930s. When a resort or other facility had one, they usually touted it with ads and postcards showing people enjoying a swim, as shown in these two views from the 1930s (above) and early 1950s (right).

Hitchin' and Tradin' Post, Highland Springs Guest Ranch, Early 1950s. By the mid-1940s, the emphasis of Highland Springs had switched to being a guest ranch. According to the card, this was where "happy guests gather to yarn, whittle sticks, and toss horse shoes. Here riders start for scenic rides over the open range . . . and through wooded canyons and mountain trails."

Lovers' Lane, Highland Springs Guest Ranch, Late 1940s. Lovers' Lane was one of many places where guests could take a stroll, ride a horse, or go for a wagon ride as this couple is doing.

HIGHLAND SPRINGS GUEST RANCH ADVERTISING CARDS, 1940S. The cartoon figures in these views are showing all of the activities available at Highland Springs. When compared to other resorts, Highland Springs did little advertising beyond postcards such as these—they relied mainly on word-of-mouth referrals from previous guests.

HOTEL EDINBURGH, 1908. The Hotel Edinburgh, located at the southeast corner of Sixth Street and Beaumont Avenue, began as the Hotel Beaumont in 1887. It closed in 1893 but was reopened in November 1907 by David Cochrane, former owner of the Hotel Holyrood in Riverside. At that time, Cochrane announced that there would be "200 feet of porches upon the roofs of which arrangements will be made for outdoor sleeping. The four acres of park surrounding the hotel already are planted to one hundred or more varieties of trees and shrubs. Tennis courts, a tea drinking pagoda, and a system of cottages for those who prefer them to rooms in the hotel are included in the plans." Unfortunately the Hotel Edinburgh burned to the ground during the night of August 17, 1909, and was not rebuilt.

SANATORIUM OF DR. JOHN KING, LATE 1910S. This facility was known officially as the Banning Hospital and Sanitarium. Dr. King was an early pioneer of Banning and served many years as its only physician. He soon realized the curative properties of Banning's climate and began promoting Banning as a center for health. In 1910, he began this sanitarium, located on Nicolet Street between Second and Third Streets (later moving it to Hoffer Street). Dr. King operated the sanitarium until he moved to Pasadena in 1923.

INTERIOR VIEW, SEYMOUR SANATORIUM, MID-1920S. Another of the several sanatoriums in Banning was the Seymour Sanatorium, originally started in 1919 by Henrietta Seymour and Mary Henderson. This building, located on George Street, underwent several owners before being closed in 1937.

HOTEL BANNING, 1929. The Hotel Banning was opened in 1929 by Guy Woodworth of the Hotel Kern near Bakersfield and his wife, Catherine. The Riverside *Daily Press* reported that it was "an up-to-date commercial hostelry . . . from the cafe and shops on the lower floor to the roof garden on the third floor." A description from the *Los Angeles Times* compares it to the missions: "There are fifty guest rooms, a lounge, a large dining-room and a coffee shop, all on the Ocean to Ocean Highway. The exterior of the building is of real Spanish style, the walls of buff stucco with overhanging roofs of red tile. A broad balcony extends across the front of the second floor, while on the ground floor a spacious veranda opens on to a patio which is filled with trees, shrubs, and flowers, giving the front of the building a most attractive and inviting appearance. The approach to the entrance is done in red tile similar to those used in the old California missions and haciendas."

HOTEL BANNING, EARLY 1940S. The Hotel Banning remained open until June 1963, when it was purchased by Pacific Homes, a Methodist nonprofit life care retirement agency. It has since changed hands, but the building is still used for a retirement home and can be seen at the northwest corner of Ramsey and Second Streets.

SAN GORGONIO INN, C. 1922. This hotel and cafe has gone through many variations throughout the years. The original town map of Banning showed the block between Ramsey, Murray, Livingstone, and Ella Streets as the hotel block. In early 1885, Banning pioneer George Bryant constructed the building shown in the center as the town's hotel. He called it the Bryant House and leased it to C. C. Henderson to operate. In 1888, Capt. Thomas Fraser and his wife, Floretta, purchased the hotel and renamed it The Banning. Captain Fraser died a few years later, but for

over 30 years, Mrs. Fraser ran The Banning. In 1920, she sold the hotel and lot to John Livacich, who refurbished the old hotel building, added bungalows on both sides of it, and renamed the new resort the San Gorgonio Inn after the pass in which it is located. Livacich's resort, as pictured above, lasted throughout the 1920s and was a primary stop for people coming to the pass to enjoy Banning's "cold mountain water, and dry desert air."

ENTRANCE TO SAN GORGONIO INN, LATE 1920S. Visible in this photograph is the old hotel building, along with some of the bungalows to the left. Situated directly on Ramsey Street (old Highway 60-70-99), the San Gorgonio Inn was a haven for both tourist and health seeker.

SAN GORGONIO INN & CAFE, C. 1932. On the night of April 14, 1930, the main building of the San Gorgonio Inn burned. Livacich rebuilt but, this time, opted for a more Spanish-style building, seen here. With several additions and modifications, this building remains today as the San Gorgonio Inn.

TWO VIEWS OF THE SAN GORGONIO INN, EARLY 1950S. By this time, more emphasis was placed on the cafe portion of the operation. The reverse of the card indicates that the inn is "famous for good food and low prices." Note the addition of the Fiesta Room on the right.

SAN GORGONIO INN SIGN, MID-1950S. For 50 years, this sign has directed people to the San Gorgonio Inn.

Four

SAN JACINTO VALLEY
AROUND SAN JACINTO AND HEMET

FARMER HOUSE, *c.* 1909. The Farmer House was a hotel near downtown San Jacinto. It was started by Jane Farmer in December 1895 in the home shown on the left. In 1898, her husband, Thomas, added the house on the right. The Farmer House was in business until 1912 when the Farmers sold the property to their daughter and son-in-law, Annie and William Vosburg.

VOSBURG HOTEL, C. 1938. From 1912 until 1971, the Vosburg Hotel was a major attraction in San Jacinto. It was advertised as being within easy reach of the many nearby hot springs resorts—Idyllwild, Riverside, and the desert resorts of Palm Springs. It was expanded over several years, ending in 1930 in the view shown here.

INTERIOR, VOSBURG HOTEL, C. 1915. This view shows the interior meeting room of the Vosburg, a staple of many hotels where guests would meet to chat. "The Hotel Vosburg is one of those well-liked country hotels with city conveniences, hot and cold water, electric lights and electric heat, cheerful lobby with big open fire-place and many easy chairs."

Overall View of Eden Hot Springs, c. 1906. Eden Hot Springs was the northernmost of the three San Jacinto–area hot springs. A resort was in place at least by 1890. In 1904, John Armstrong bought the springs and began construction of the facilities shown in this card, namely a small hotel and several guest cottages. Over the next 30 years, Eden Hot Springs continued to attract visitors for its healing waters. In 1930, a modern Spanish-style building was constructed, but it lasted only a few years. During the 1930s, all of the hot springs in the San Jacinto area dried up, and Eden Hot Springs, set in the hills instead of on the main road, was soon forgotten.

HOTEL, EDEN HOT SPRINGS, *c.* 1908. Typically most hot springs resorts had both cabins and a hotel, the latter for guests who did not want to "camp out." At the time of this picture, the hotel was small in nature but comfortable enough for the two guests shown here.

COTTAGE ROW AND BATHHOUSES, EDEN HOT SPRINGS, *c.* 1908. Note here the cistern to the left, the bathhouse beyond it, and a few of the cabins available to guests farther down. On the right are changing rooms.

TYPICAL COTTAGE, EDEN HOT SPRINGS, *c.* 1908. When people came to resorts such as Eden Hot Springs, it was usually for a stay of several weeks. Many people established a home away from home in one of the small cabins such as the one pictured above.

WATER CISTERN, EDEN HOT SPRINGS, *c.* 1908. Most hot springs resorts had open reservoirs so that people could enjoy the waters at all times. In typical advertising jargon of the time, this postcard boasts that "Our mud and tub sulphur baths stand second to none in the cure of Rheumatism, Eczema, Stomach and Kidney troubles."

SAN JACINTO HOT SPRINGS, C. 1908. These hot springs were located northwest of San Jacinto and were the precursor to Gilman Hot Springs. Known for several thousand years by the local American Indians, these hot springs were bought and developed into a resort by Sidney Branch of Riverside in 1885. In 1888, the hotel building pictured above was constructed by Branch. For the most part, the Branch family owned the hot springs and resort until 1913, when they sold the facility to W. Earl Gilman and his two brothers, Grant and Forest. The Gilman family owned and further developed the property until 1978.

BACKSIDE OF SAN JACINTO HOT SPRINGS BUILDING, C. 1912. This view shows the far side of the hotel building seen in the previous view (left) and some of the cottages that could also be rented. "Came over from Murrieta Hot Springs by Otto (sic) today—the trip through the mountains and valley was beautiful."

BATHHOUSES, SAN JACINTO HOT SPRINGS, C. 1908. As always, the bathhouses were separate from the hotel. This view shows the bathhouses in existence at the time of the Branch family ownership. It was later described as "a sad looking building—rough wood inside and out—the tule mud in wooden tubs and the rinsing water in rough, corroded metal tubs. It was most necessary to step in with caution for fear of abrading the skin."

MAIN BUILDING, GILMAN'S RELIEF HOT SPRINGS, MID-1920S. In 1913, the Gilman brothers bought the resort from the Branch family and immediately began making improvements. One improvement was forced upon them—the building above. In February 1918, the main hotel building and several cottages burned. Just a few months later, a large earthquake wreaked havoc in San Jacinto. Due to the shortage of building materials in World War I, the Gilmans rebuilt the hotel (pictured above) with bricks recovered from the San Jacinto School. This picture shows the main entryway and parking lot, with the lobby and portions of the resort behind.

PORTION OF THE LOBBY, GILMAN HOT SPRINGS, MID-1920S. The lobby of the hotel acted as hotel reception area and meeting area. This view shows the grand fireplace with hunting trophies depicting the kinds of game available to hunters. Also shown are plenty of tables and rocking chairs for guests as well as a small store stocking many of life's necessities, including, no doubt, postcards such as this one.

GUESTS AT BLACK SULPHUR SPRINGS, GILMAN'S RELIEF HOT SPRINGS, LATE 1910S. Four main springs were found on the property—Black Sulphur, White Sulphur, Soda, and Lithia. Here several guests partake of the waters. "The black sulphur water which gushes from these springs is of benefit in cases of gout, rheumatism and skin diseases," reported one advertisement.

HOTEL BUILDING AND COTTAGES, GILMAN'S RELIEF HOT SPRINGS, C. 1920. The main hotel building is clearly visible here in the center. In the foreground are several of the rebuilt cottages. Typically, resorts such as Gilman's had several different types of facilities in which people could stay, to accommodate a wide range of tastes.

COTTAGES AT GILMAN'S HOT SPRINGS, C. 1920. In the early years, Gilman's Hot Springs developed more cottages than any other type of facility—mainly because that's what the public demanded. Note here the open spaces in front of the cottages. Walking and hiking were popular pastimes while staying at resorts like these, and with more than 150 acres, Gilman's could accommodate those pedestrian guests.

NEW ANNEX BUILDING, GILMAN'S RELIEF HOT SPRINGS, EARLY 1920S. This new building was added to the grounds in 1920–1921 and brought 50 new rooms to the resort. At this point, Gilman's was being advertised as "the ALL YEAR RESORT where the sick can be won back to health and where those in health can keep that way."

NEW BATHHOUSE ADDITION, GILMAN'S HOT SPRINGS, MID-1920S. This new bathhouse was completed sometime in the mid-1920s and offered the most modern accommodations for people wanting to enjoy the sulphur and mud baths offered. Note the hills in the background—most of the views of hot springs resorts are shown with hills since most hot springs are located along fault lines.

Swimming Pool, Gilman's Relief Hot Springs, Early 1920s. Constructed in 1914, the swimming pool was one of the earliest improvements to the resort. Around 1920, it was enclosed and offered guests what was at the time an unusual opportunity—to swim in a pool. As in many hot springs resorts, the pool would have been filled with mineral water.

Tennis Courts, Gilman's Relief Hot Springs, Early 1920s. Exercise was stressed at many of the hot springs resorts as a way of helping to recuperate. As tennis was becoming popular at the time, Gilman's installed the tennis courts seen above where, as the card says, pleasant times were to be had.

CAFETERIA DINING ROOM, GILMAN'S HOT SPRINGS, MID-1920S. Although Gilman's started out offering the American Plan wherein guests received their meals in a more traditional sit-down environment, this changed in 1922 when the old way was dropped and the cafeteria shown above was added. All guests' meals were served here throughout their stay at the resort.

DANCE HALL, GILMAN'S RELIEF HOT SPRINGS, *C.* 1925. Dances were popular forms of entertainment in the days before television, so most resorts had dance halls and some form of musical entertainment. At Gilman's, dances were held Friday nights with music furnished by a piano player, violinist, and drummer, most of whom were staff members.

LADIES' PARLOR, GILMAN HOT SPRINGS, LATE 1920S. This large room served as a separate meeting and relaxation room for the female guests of the resort.

COCKTAIL ROOM, GILMAN HOT SPRINGS, MID-1930S. After the repeal of prohibition, resorts in general added bars and lounges to accommodate the guests who wanted to socialize over a good stiff drink, and Gilman's was no exception. Note the old jukebox on the left and the caption indicating that the cocktail room is air-conditioned—a true rarity in the mid-1930s.

PEOPLE LOUNGING AT GILMAN HOT SPRINGS, MID-1940S. In an era when people regularly worked six and seven days per week, the ability to take a vacation and simply relax was quite an amenity, as pictured in this postcard of people taking it easy at Gilman's. This was epitomized by one guest who wrote, "We are up here for a couple of weeks sojourn and love it—warm as summer, sitting in patio after sulphur bath—right in the mountains." Another indicated that he was "up here boiling out for a couple weeks—great place, feel fine."

PORTIONS OF ORIGINAL GOLF COURSE, GILMAN HOT SPRINGS, MID-1930S. This nine-hole golf course was added in 1930 and became an immediate attraction. Over the years, it was expanded several times, and it continues to be a major attraction under the Golden Era moniker.

GOLF COURSE, GILMAN HOT SPRINGS, EARLY 1960S. By the time this view was captured, the golf course had become part of a later Gilman incarnation known as the Massacre Canyon Inn. Named for a nearby canyon (see next page), the new name never really took hold, always being secondary to Gilman Hot Springs.

MASSACRE CANYON, NEAR GILMAN HOT SPRINGS, *c.* 1908. Massacre Canyon was a popular hiking and riding destination less than a mile from the main Gilman resort. It provided a great place for picnics or other outings. Guests were always surprised by the lush vegetation so near the hotel.

MASSACRE CANYON FALLS, GILMAN HOT SPRINGS, *c.* 1920. Massacre Canyon has extremely steep walls, and dead-ends at this spring-fed fall. According to local American Indian lore, the name comes from a time when most of the men of the village of Ivah, where Gilman Hot Springs is located, were killed in this canyon during a battle for food with other American Indians from Temecula.

HOTEL BUILDING, SOBOBA HOT SPRINGS, LATE 1910S. By at least 1883, Dr. B. A. Wright had started San Jacinto Sulphur Springs, the third hot springs resort in the vicinity of San Jacinto. By 1899, it had become run down. In that year, Col. James Ritchey bought the property and developed it into Soboba Hot Springs, naming it for the nearby Soboba Indians. At that time, he built the hotel shown above as the main building at Soboba. Colonel Ritchey owned the resort until his death in 1908, and his family owned it for a few more years after that. However, the main development of Soboba Hot Springs came under the direction of John and Tillie Althouse, who arrived in 1919 to manage the resort, purchasing it in 1924. They owned Soboba for nearly 30 years.

GROUNDS, SOBOBA HOT SPRINGS, *C.* 1917. Much of the resort is obscured by the landscaping, but in this view, the main building is visible just to the right of center, as are many of the individual frame cottages that were the mainstay of the resort in its early years. Note the fruit orchard in the foreground. Fresh, healthy food was a must at resorts catering to "reviving" a person.

ENTRANCE TO SOBOBA HOT SPRINGS, *C.* 1917. At left is the larger building identifiable in the postcard above. If the ladies posing for this picture were from the Midwest or East Coast, it may have been their first chance to see the "tropical" pepper trees in the background.

RESTFUL SPOT, SOBOBA HOT SPRINGS, *c.* 1912. "Soboba Hot Springs Resort is open year 'round . . . a delightful place to come at any season . . . a healthful spot where you can rest, play, enjoy life, and improve your health through wholesome, outdoor exercise, and healthful mineral water treatments. When you come to Soboba, comfort and simplicity, wholesomeness, and cordial hospitality await you. You will feel at once the soothing spell of the hills. You will take deep full breaths of the pure mountain air, relax, expand, enjoy to the fullest the rare contentment and serenity of life in these peaceful hills."

VIEW OF SAN JACINTO VALLEY, SOBOBA HOT SPRINGS, *C.* 1912. The fact that Soboba lay in the San Jacinto Valley, the "Heart of Ramonaland" as it was known, did not escape the boosters of the resort. They wrote, "Rich is the history of Soboba Springs, filled with the glamour and romance of early California days, when the Indians roamed the rugged hills and green plains of San Jacinto, and came to rest and bathe at these springs of natural healthfulness. Here great fiestas were held in the days of the *Indian* and the *Don*; here is laid part of the famous novel, 'Ramona'; and here Ramona and Alessandro, and their ancestors for generations before them, sought health and relief in the beneficial waters."

View of Cottages, Soboba Hot Springs, c. 1912. These frame cottages were typical of many resorts of the time. "The frame cottages are large, roomy, and above the quality usually found, and have running water, electric lights, and stoves for heating. Large screened canvas windows provide ample ventilation. They are pleasantly situated among palms and pepper trees, which furnish shade in the summer time."

Eucalyptus Drive, Soboba Hot Springs, c. 1920. Peaceful walkways with tropical vegetation, in this case eucalyptus and citrus, were always popular in Southern California. Here three ladies take a stroll in the relaxing atmosphere at Soboba.

HOLLOW TILE COTTAGE, SOBOBA HOT SPRINGS, SAN JACINTO, CAL.

VIEWS OF HOLLOW TILE COTTAGES, SOBOBA HOT SPRINGS, *C.* 1912. These cottages were some of the "midrange" accommodations that awaited guests at Soboba and were described as "large, well ventilated and comfortably furnished. They have hot and cold running water, electric lights, shower baths and toilets, and stoves for heating in cooler weather." Hollow-tile construction had one other advantage too—it was very fireproof, which was a major consideration in construction and advertising at that time.

INTERIOR VIEW OF TILE COTTAGE SOBOBA HOT SPRINGS, SAN JACINTO, CAL.

INDIAN VILLAGE, SOBOBA HOT SPRINGS, C. 1928. Around 1927, Althouse added the most defining feature of Soboba Hot Springs—the Indian Village. Designed by Los Angeles architect R. B. Stacy-Judd, these 14 cottages were constructed using features he had seen in American Indian architecture of the Southwest. All of them featured American Indian names such as Yuma, Pima, Maricopa, etc. Yuma stands in the right foreground. "Like a scene from some fantasy of long ago, they stand in the serene peace of the majestic mountains . . . their colorful tiles and pottery gleaming in the sunlight. The Indian lodges are in perfect harmony with the rugged setting and romantic history of Soboba Springs."

Shasta Indian Lodge, Soboba Hot Springs, c. 1928. Some of the wealthier guests would bring their own physicians with them when they came to Soboba. One doctor wrote, "Isn't this a beautiful place? My patient is taking treatments here. We will be here 2 weeks. I am having a real vacation, and it doesn't cost me anything."

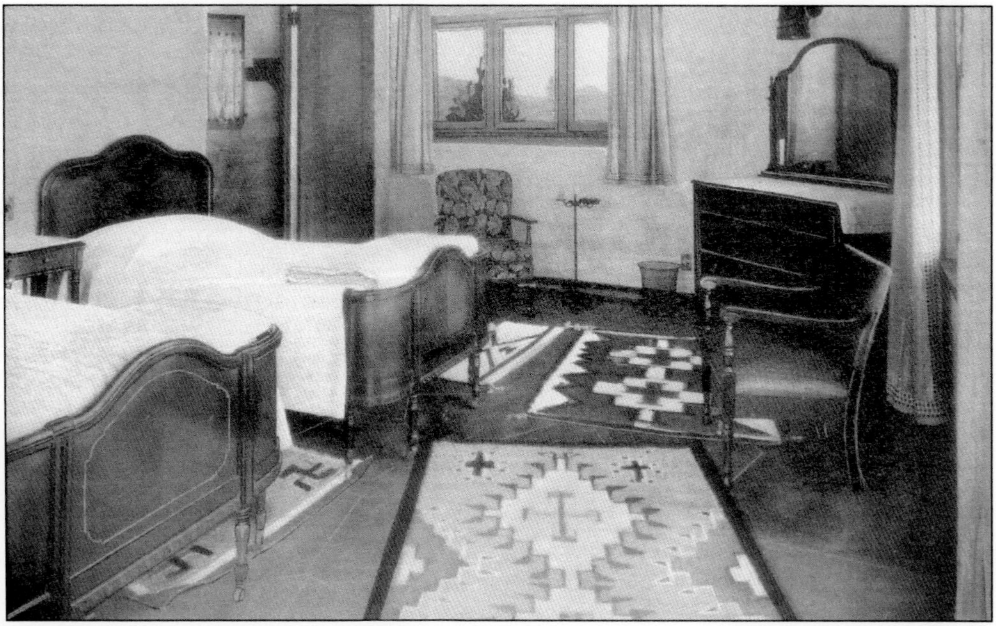

Interior of Yuma Indian Lodge, Soboba Hot Springs, c. 1930. An early advertising brochure enticed prospective guests by stating the following: "Every possible comfort and convenience has been incorporated into these attractive guest quarters. The rough Indian architecture of their exteriors gives way, upon entering, to beautifully appointed rooms and suites. The Indian motif is carried out in the appropriately decorated walls, curtains, and hand-wrought lamp shades, hardware, and fittings."

SOBOBA BATHS, SOBOBA HOT SPRINGS. SAN JACINTO, CALIFORNIA.

BATHHOUSE, SOBOBA HOT SPRINGS, LATE 1920S. Situated with a grand view of the San Jacinto Valley, the bathhouse at Soboba was the main attraction for people coming to the resort. "[I]t fairly radiates cleanliness, sunshine and sanitation. The equipment includes approved modern appliances and conveniences of every type. Large and comfortable lobbies, sun rooms, complete facilities for baths of every type, dressing rooms for outdoor bathers are included." In 1930, the bathhouse offered everything from a mineral bath for 50¢ to a "blood wash" for $10.

MIRROR POOL, SOBOBA HOT SPRINGS, LATE 1920S. The mirror pool held mineral water taken from the springs and served as the main swimming pool for guests at Soboba. "The Soboba waters have a soft velvety feeling that is very soothing to the skin and nerves and after a bath, one feels rested, refreshed, and exhilarated," wrote one promotional brochure around 1930.

RAMADA, SOBOBA HOT SPRINGS, EARLY 1920S. Many health seekers coming to Southern California did so because of the climate. Therefore, many of the activities, be they active or passive, were planned outdoors. Note in this view the various chairs, card tables, gramophone, swing, and other amenities that allowed guests to enjoy Soboba's climate.

CANYON OF SPRINGS, SOBOBA HOT SPRINGS, *C.* 1920. The actual springs that supplied Soboba Hot Springs with its water were located up a small canyon behind the resort. This area was landscaped and guests could stroll to see the springs that fed Soboba.

SPRING, SOBOBA HOT SPRINGS, LATE 1920S. The springs themselves were quite an attraction, so the resort owners developed the area around them for peaceful contemplation. Their existence, and the reason for their temperature and mineral content, is due to their location along the San Jacinto fault.

KEN KREIGH ROCK GARDEN DESIGNS, SOBOBA HOT SPRINGS, LATE 1930S. Ken Kreigh was a local rock garden designer who was hired by the Althouses to design a patio area for the resort. This creation became famous in its own right and made for a relaxing guest area just near the main hotel building. While Kreigh was constructing the garden, using rock from the Searl Ranch in Diamond Valley, he was visited often by actress Jean Harlow, one of the many Hollywood stars to frequent these and other hot springs resorts in their heyday.

TWO VIEWS OF THE HOTEL HEMET, *C.* 1910. The Hotel Hemet began in 1894 as the Hotel Mayberry, named for Edward L. Mayberry, one of the founders of the town. Located at the southeast corner of Florida Avenue and State Street, it had 36 rooms and was plainly visible from the depot across the street. In 1898, the other principal behind Hemet, William Whittier, took over the hotel and renamed it the Hotel Hemet. Whittier renovated it after the 1899 San Jacinto earthquake caused substantial damage. This building burned in March 1917, and it was decided by Whittier's heirs not to rebuild, since the hotel had not been profitable.

HOTEL ALESSANDRO, MID-1930s. The Hotel Alessandro opened in March 1929 on the same location as the old Hotel Hemet. It had 60 rooms, a patio, dining room, and coffee shop. Designed by Edward L Mayberry Jr., it cost $125,000 to build and was constructed in a pueblo style that was sweeping the Hemet–San Jacinto area at the time.

HOTEL ALESSANDRO, LATE 1940s. By this time, the palm trees had grown substantially, and more of the building could be seen. However, the Hotel Alessandro would not last much longer—it was torn down in 1953 to make way for a bank.

HOTEL ALESSANDRO, MID-1940S. The Hotel Alessandro was named for the hero in Helen Hunt Jackson's famous novel *Ramona.* With the beginning of the Ramona Pageant in 1923, the whole San Jacinto Valley embraced the Ramona story and myth, and many places were either named for characters in the book or designed in a manner to reflect Ramona. Although *Ramona* was fiction, it had a powerful influence on the valley and, in general, Southern California.

INDIAN PATIO, HOTEL ALESSANDRO, LATE 1930S. It seemed only fitting that a hotel named for an American Indian (albeit fictional) should have an Indian Patio on which to relax. This view shows the Indian Patio at the Hotel Alessandro, designed to resemble the American Indian villages that had dotted the San Jacinto Valley for many generations.

Five

San Jacinto Mountains
Idyllwild and Vicinity

Idyllwild Area, 1930s. Since at least the 1870s, the San Jacinto Mountains area of the county offered a pleasant place for a getaway from the heat. Many different resorts operated and continue to operate today, catering to those who want to escape to the mountains, if only for a little while.

IDYLLWILD SANITARIUM, *C.* 1902. The Idyllwild Sanitarium began as a project of the California Health Resort Company, led by Drs. Walter Lindley and F. T. Bicknell. Construction began in 1900, and it opened in June 1901. This sanitarium catered to patients with tuberculosis but was never much of a success due to the colder climate in the mountains. In July 1903, it closed and soon reopened as the Strawberry Valley Hotel, catering to healthy vacationers instead. However, less than a year later, the building was destroyed by fire. A new building was then built on its location. That building, initially called The Bungalow, would later become the Idyllwild Inn.

IDYLLWILD INN, 1920S. By the time of this photograph, the Idyllwild Inn had come into the possession of a syndicate known as Idyllwild Incorporated, headed by Claudius Lee Emerson. Emerson did his utmost to make Idyllwild a popular resort area, catering to those who wished to vacation in the mile-high area. In addition to the building shown here, there were several outlying cabins, and eventually tennis courts and a golf course.

IDYLLWILD INN, LATE 1940S. In May 1945, the original Idyllwild Inn burned to the ground. It was rebuilt a year later, as shown in the above view. This building continued to welcome guests for another 30 years under several different owners, but it was demolished in 1976 when it was no longer a profitable venture.

VIEW OF COTTAGES, IDYLLWILD, 1908. The cottages seen here began as part of the Idyllwild Sanitarium, then the Strawberry Valley Hotel, and finally the Idyllwild Inn. Horseback riding or, in this girl's case, burro riding were very popular pastimes for guests at many of the mountain resorts. Trips to San Jacinto peak, Tahquitz peak, or other locations offered day- or overnight trips.

STRAWBERRY CREEK, IDYLLWILD, MID-1920S. The Idyllwild area was originally known as Strawberry Valley due to the large amount of wild strawberries growing there. The creek that ran through it was similarly named Strawberry Creek. This was a popular place for rest, relaxation, and of course, postcards.

IDYLLWILD BUSINESS CENTER, LATE 1940S. In the 1920s, the town of Idyllwild came into existence. Large landowners believed that people would not only want to visit Idyllwild for a vacation but potentially live there as well. They were right. Many people began to purchase lots and build mostly summer homes in the region. The town of Idyllwild itself became a resort, with many additional lodges, cabins, etc. being built to accommodate the growing number of visitors. This view shows the small business district that sprang up. Gray's Souvenirs and Woodland Crafts is in the center.

KEEN CAMP, *C.* 1930. Around 1905, Keen Camp was started by John and Mary Keen. The Keens were already well-known mountain area hosts, having run the Keen House for several years. Keen Camp had its own lodge and cabins, and catered to vacationers. In 1911, the Keens sold the property to Percy and Anita Walker.

TAHQUITZ LODGE, KEEN CAMP, *C.* 1930. In 1919, the widowed Anita Walker remarried, and the new couple renamed Keen Camp the Tahquitz Lodge, adding more cabins and a swimming pool. Tahquitz Lodge, named for the spirit who inhabited the San Jacinto Mountains, became popular in its own right but was always second to the Idyllwild Inn.

TAHQUITZ LODGE VIEWS, 1920S. These two views show the relaxing atmosphere at the Tahquitz Lodge. Unfortunately the lodge underwent a transformation in 1924 when it was bought and converted into a private club. The club was very unsuccessful, and it was returned to the previous owner. Business did not pick up during the 1930s, despite best efforts. In November 1943, the entire lodge and several cabins were lost to a devastating fire, from which the owners could not recover. Tahquitz Lodge was closed forever.

Scene on Road to Idyllwild, Riverside Co., Cal.

ROAD TO IDYLLWILD, *C.* 1912. Just getting to the Idyllwild area in the early years was cause for concern, so some people took it upon themselves to mail postcards showing the route, like the one above. Generally one took a wagon not unlike that shown here, left Hemet in the morning, and arrived at Idyllwild some five to six hours later. Undoubtedly this view was taken to show that the road was not too steep (at least here!) and could be navigated with little trouble. Over the years, the road was greatly improved, and additional roads, leading to Banning and eventually Palm Desert, were added to facilitate greater access to "the hill."

Six

Coachella Valley

Palm Springs, Desert Hot Springs, Indio, and La Quinta

Agua Caliente Bathhouse, Palm Springs, *c.* 1920. This view shows the Agua Caliente bathhouse, constructed in 1916, over the springs for which Palm Springs is named. Local American Indians had refreshed themselves in the springs for centuries by the time of the first commercial use of the springs in the 1880s. Today this area is the known as the Spa Resort and Casino in downtown Palm Springs.

Entrance, the Desert Inn, Late 1920s. The Desert Inn was the premier resort in Palm Springs for much of the early 20th century. Started by Nellie Coffman in 1909 as a small tent-house resort, it soon grew in size and stature. By the 1920s, it was well known throughout the country, catering to a diverse crowd ranging from vacationers to the wealthy who wanted to remain anonymous.

Main Building, The Desert Inn, 1933. In October 1926, the main lobby building shown here was opened, adding a Spanish-style lobby, entrance, and dining room. This building became the hallmark of the Desert Inn and hosted numerous gatherings. Note the number of automobiles in the parking lot. By this time, Palm Springs could be reached by paved highway from Banning—a true asset!

BUNGALOW AND CANAL, THE DESERT INN, 1937. This bungalow was one of approximately 35 buildings that comprised the Desert Inn and was available for guests who wanted more privacy. The canal seen here belonged to the Agua Caliente Indians and brought water from Tahquitz Canyon to their lands in downtown Palm Springs.

SWIMMING POOL, THE DESERT INN, 1947. This swimming pool was the first in Palm Springs, and was originally used as a small reservoir for irrigation water. Soon though, it was converted into a swimming pool and became a very popular place for cooling off in the desert. The building in the upper left is the Desert Inn's honeymoon cottage.

LODGE NO. 1 (TOP) AND LODGE NO. 2, THE DESERT INN, *c.* 1930. These two lodges, located behind the main lobby building, represented some of the better accommodations at the Desert Inn. Lodge No. 2 housed the first elevator in Palm Springs. In 1934, one guest noted that "we motored here from Los Angeles 120 miles to spend a day. It is a very charming spot, and much patronized by movie stars."

EARLY VIEW, THE DESERT INN, C. 1920. This view shows one of the original buildings that belonged to Lavinia Crocker, who ran a sanitarium on the property prior to the Coffman's purchase. The building is right along Palm Canyon Drive, and the view is to the northwest. In later years, this building was used as the main office, and still later as housing for the several Filipino employees who served as waiters, busboys, and kitchen help.

El Mirador Hotel, Palm Springs, 1933. The El Mirador opened on January 1, 1928, to great fanfare. It was to be a first-class luxury hotel and was touted as "another of those miracles of the desert which is fast transforming the vast expanse of sand-bound waste into spots of beauty." The building was constructed in only 18 weeks by a consortium led by Prescott T. Stevens.

Gardens, El Mirador Hotel, c. 1929. Los Angeles horticulturist O. W. Howard made many trips to the deserts of California and Arizona, where he collected specimens of desert cacti to be placed in the gardens of the El Mirador. When the hotel opened, it was stated that $75,000 was being spent on the gardens alone, and that they would be a place of instruction as well as relaxation.

VIEW FROM THE BELL TOWER, EL MIRADOR HOTEL, *c.* 1930. These ladies are looking out over the desert and mountains from the El Mirador's famed bell tower, which housed a bell imported from the Church of Our Lady of Amalfi, Italy. The hotel boasted 200 rooms, plus all of the fineries that could be had at the time. Unfortunately the hotel opened near the beginning of the Great Depression and suffered throughout the 1930s. Today it is the site of the Desert Regional Medical Center.

HOTEL DEL TAHQUITZ, 1936. The Hotel del Tahquitz was built by movie star Fritzi Ridgeway on property at the corner of Palm Canyon Drive and Baristo Street. Because she was intrigued by American Indian architecture, Ridgeway built the del Tahquitz in the pueblo style she had seen throughout the Southwest.

HOTEL DEL TAHQUITZ, 1947. Opened on November 28, 1929, the del Tahquitz was named for Tahquitz Canyon that lay less than a half mile to the west. The hotel sported many statues and other works of American Indian art that Fritzi Ridgeway had found on her travels throughout the Southwest.

COURTYARD OF THE HOTEL DEL TAHQUITZ, 1933. According to the *Los Angeles Times*, "The hotel has 100 all-outside rooms constructed about a giant patio, which Miss Ridgeway plans to transform into a huge desert garden with all sorts of tropical trees and desert flora incorporated in picturesque fashion. The patio also is to have a large swimming pool."

SIDE VIEW, HOTEL DEL TAHQUITZ, MID-1940S. Although the del Tahquitz played host to many well-known celebrities in its day, by the late 1950s its luster had apparently worn off. By 1958, a proposal was initiated to demolish the hotel and replace it with a new, modern bowling alley.

HOTEL THE OASIS, LATE 1920S. The Oasis opened in 1925 on grounds that had been owned by Palm Springs founder John Guthrie McCallum. Not only was the Oasis described as a fine hotel, but it boasted a Persian-style swimming pool and an extensive garden designed by Lloyd Wright, son of famed designer Frank Lloyd Wright.

THE ADOBE, HOTEL THE OASIS, LATE 1920S. The Oasis was built around the original adobe home of John McCallum. This small structure was kept in place on the grounds of the Oasis as a memorial to him by his daughter Pearl McCallum McManus. In later years, this adobe was moved closer to the shopping district on Palm Canyon Drive, and today serves as the museum for the Palm Springs Historical Society.

DESERT HOT SPRINGS MINERAL BATHHOUSE, DESERT HOT SPRINGS, EARLY 1950S. Desert Hot Springs was started as a resort town by L. W. Coffee. In the 1930s, Coffee began drilling wells north of Palm Springs in search of water. What he found was naturally occurring mineral water—enough to develop a community. With financial backing, he bought land, subdivided lots, and began the Mineral Bathhouse shown above in July 1941. Desert Hot Springs thrived after the war, appealing to people who wanted to live in a community based upon the healing properties of the nearby natural mineral water.

INTERIOR VIEW, MINERAL BATHHOUSE, DESERT HOT SPRINGS, MID-1940S. In the early years of Desert Hot Springs, L. W. Coffee's mineral bathhouse was the main attraction. This postcard shows the main building above and, below, the sweat cots on the right and the specially designed mineral bath tubs on the left.

INTERIOR VIEW, MINERAL BATHHOUSE, DESERT HOT SPRINGS, MID-1940S. This view is the opposite of the one above. Here, we see a better view of the mineral bath tubs plus two attendants preparing to give a massage to a client in the special massage room.

Val Samuelson Cartoon Postcards, Desert Hot Springs, 1953. These two advertising cards sought to show would-be visitors the pleasures of basking in the sun and pools of Desert Hot Springs. The cartoons were drawn by renowned desert-area artist Val Samuelson. (Reproduced with permission from Marion Samuelson).

AERIAL VIEW, SHADOW MOUNTAIN CLUB, LATE 1940S. In December 1948, the Shadow Mountain Club opened in the newly developed town of Palm Desert. It was a full resort, with tennis, golf, a boating lake, and of course, a swimming pool.

FIGURE 8 SWIMMING POOL, SHADOW MOUNTAIN CLUB, 1949. A unique feature of the Shadow Mountain Club, both in 1949 and today, is the figure-eight swimming pool. During the post-war era, many hotels and resorts were adding swimming pools to their list of attractions, and the Shadow Mountain Club pool's unique shape was another lure to attract tourists.

OUTDOOR DINING TERRACE, SHADOW MOUNTAIN CLUB, 1949. This postcard indicates that the club was "in a perfect setting with a panoramic view of the snow-capped peaks of Mt. San Jacinto and San Gorgonio on the west, the unspoiled desert on the north, date gardens to the east and the majestic Santa Rosa mountains on the south. It is truly a vista that is unsurpassed."

BOATING AND SAILING LAKE, SHADOW MOUNTAIN CLUB, EARLY 1950S. Imagine the surprise awaiting visitors to the Shadow Mountain Club when they came upon a boating lake in the middle of the desert.

OVERALL VIEW OF LA QUINTA HOTEL, 1930S. On January 29, 1927, the La Quinta Hotel opened to a full crowd of patrons and dinner guests. Built by William Morgan and designed by Gordon Kaufman, the La Quinta Hotel soon came to epitomize the out-of-the-way desert retreat. The hotel consisted of several small casitas, which offered privacy to all guests. Morgan began to market the hotel to Hollywood stars and business tycoons, and soon La Quinta became discreetly known for its clientele. Except for a closure during World War II, the La Quinta Hotel has remained open throughout the years and continues to attract people today as the La Quinta Resort and Club.

Main Building, La Quinta Hotel, 1930s. The La Quinta Hotel was built in the style of a Mexican country home surrounded by smaller casitas. It was built entirely of adobe bricks made onsite, as were the roof and floor tiles.

View of Interior Courtyard, La Quinta Hotel, Early 1930s. This view was probably meant to emphasize the abundant sunshine, enveloping mountains, and Spanish architecture that combined to make La Quinta Hotel the secluded "getaway" place for which it was famous. Since climate was a major attraction to the desert, the La Quinta Hotel offered an open-air courtyard, as seen here.

LOGGIA AND BUNGALOW, LA QUINTA HOTEL, EARLY 1930S. Many early postcard views of hotels such as La Quinta emphasized the openness, sunshine, and flowers that would greet the prospective guest. To a prospective clientele situated in a harsh winter environment, views such as these did much to attract them to come west.

DINING ROOM, LA QUINTA HOTEL, LATE 1920S. Gordon Kaufman designed not only the building but also the furniture and other intricacies of the hotel. This view of the La Mirage Dining Room showed prospective guests what awaited them during their stay.

La Quinta Hotel Pool, Late 1930s. The pool was added in 1937 as another attraction of the hotel. Many finer hotels of the period were adding pools for the enjoyment of their guests at a time when swimming pools were a very special amenity. La Quinta Hotel guests were also treated to a real date garden, as seen in the upper right.

Main Entrance, La Quinta Hotel, Early 1950s. This view shows the portion of the hotel that greeted guests as they first arrived. By this time, the hotel was still listed as being located "near Indio."

INDIO DEPOT, 1910S. For several years, the Southern Pacific depot at Indio also housed a rough resort/hotel of sorts, catering to health seekers coming to the desert. Indio's climate had been touted as far back as 1891, when Dr. Walter Lindley wrote that "the combination of aridity and high altitude injures the person suffering from overwork and nervous trouble, while the aridity with a low altitude soothes and rests, and thus benefits those who have been suffering from a nervous strain. The physician who has a patient suffering from insomnia can conscientiously send him to Indio. The nights are most delightful. It is the usual plan of the hotel to throw open all the windows and doors and practically sleep outside, and yet no person catches cold. The consumptive, who along the coast finds it necessary to protect himself from the night air, can sleep out with impunity. The physicians recommending patients to try Indio should caution them to first secure accommodations at the hotel, because there is always a far greater demand than they have room for."

HOTEL INDIO, MID-1920s. The Hotel Indio was opened in 1925 by E. R. Cooper. Hoping to attract people to the desert climate, Cooper advertised the hotel as being in the "Heart of the Coachella Valley." The building was located at the corner of Smurr Street and Miles Avenue on a parcel that had been one of Indio's first trash dumps.

HOTEL INDIO, LATE 1930s. The building housed 60 rooms, of which 40 had private bathrooms. As was typical of better hotels of the period, a garden-like courtyard greeted visitors and acted as a place for get-togethers and quiet repose. Unfortunately, in 2004, the Hotel Indio burned to the ground.

Bibliography

Bogert, Frank M. *Palm Springs: First Hundred Years (Revised Edition)*. Palm Springs, California: Palm Springs Public Library, 2003.

Brigandi, Phil. *Temecula—At the Crossroads of History*. Encinitas, California: Heritage Media Corporation, 1998.

Cobb, Sue, Ron Snow, and Linda Bruinsma. *Norco Remembers*. Norco, California: The Citizens of Norco, 1989.

Desert Sun, various dates.

Elsinore *Leader-Press*, various dates.

Gabbert, John. *History of Riverside City and County*. Riverside, California: Record Publishing Company, 1935.

Garrison, Arlean V. *My Children's Home—A History of Murrieta, California*. Elsinore, California: Mayhall Print Shop, 1963.

Gunther, Jane Davies. *Riverside County, California Place Names*. Riverside, California: Rubidoux Printing Company, 1984.

Hemet-San Jacinto Genealogical Society. *San Jacinto Valley: Past and Present*. Dallas, Texas: Curtis Media Corporation, 1989.

Hudson, Tom. *Lake Elsinore Valley: Its Story 1776–1977*. Lake Elsinore, California: Laguna House, 1978.

Hughes, Tom. *History of Banning and San Gorgonio Pass*. Banning, California: Banning Record Print, 1938.

Hunt, John J. *The Waters of Comfort*. Desert Hot Springs, California: Little Morongo Press, 1997.

Knight, Lilah Merrifield. "Lake Elsinore Historical Society Docent Training Class Notes."

La Quinta Historical Society. *The History of La Quinta—The Gem of the Desert*. La Quinta, California: La Quinta Historical Society, 1990.

La Quinta Resort and Club. *La Quinta Resort and Club History*. La Quinta Resort and Club: (nd).

Lech, Steve. *Along the Old Roads—A History of the Portion of Southern California That Became Riverside County, 1772–1893*. Riverside, California: Published by the author, 2004.

———. *Riverside in Vintage Postcards*. San Francisco, California: Arcadia Publishing, 2005.

Lindley, Walter. "Indio—The Colorado Desert for Health." *New York Medical Record*. New York, New York: 1894.

Los Angeles Times, various dates.

Pinto, Diana G. *If Stones Could Talk*. Upland, California: Dragonflyer Press, 2003.

Rail-Boyce, Mary Alice. *Murrieta: Old Town, New Town*. Murrieta, California: Rosemar Publishing Company, 1995.

Riverside County Chamber of Commerce. "Riverside County—Its Hotels and Resorts." Riverside, California: Riverside County Chamber of Commerce, (n.d., probably 1930).

Riverside *Daily Press*, various dates.

Robinson, John W. and Bruce D. Risher. *The San Jacintos*. Arcadia, California: Big Santa Anita Historical Society, 1993.

Parker, Horace. *The First Sixty Years: Guenther's Murrieta Hot Springs*. Corona del Mar, California: Hendricks Printing Company, 1961.

Soboba Mineral Hot Springs. Soboba Hot Springs. (n.d., probably 1930.)

Tapper, Violet, and Nellie Lolmaugh. *The Friendliest Valley*. Hemet, California: Hungry Eye Books, 1971.

Whitney, Mary E. *Valley, River and Mountain*. Hemet, California: Hemet Area Museum, 1999.